FENG SHUI
& YOUR HOME

GW00514674

Nightingale

An imprint of Wimbledon Publishing Company
LONDON

Copyright © 2000
Illustrations © 2000 WPC

First published in Great Britain in 2000
by Wimbledon Publishing Company Ltd
P.O. Box 9779 London SW19 7ZG
All rights reserved

First published 2000 in Great Britain

ISBN: 1903222 14 1

Produced in Great Britain
Printed and bound in Hungary

LIFE IS WORTH LIVING IF YOU MAKE IT
MORE BEAUTIFUL THAN WHEN YOU
FOUND IT.

-Frank Lloyd Wright

I have written this little book to give you some tips for living in peace and harmony. The fluctuating energy forces around you influence your physical, mental and emotional well-being. The balance between your inner and outer energy forces determines your level of happiness. Your home is a link in this process, as it is an extension of you - a third layer after your skin and clothes.

Our understanding of this has created the body of knowledge we call 'interior design', which helps create a home that is comfortable, practical and aesthetically pleasing.

This book takes this practice a step further. By weaving the principles of Feng Shui into your interior design, it points you in the direction of calm and serene living. It will change your inner landscape by changing your outer one.

Read it, enjoy it and transform your life.

Aroon Ajmera
1999

Ch'i and Feng Shui

The direct translation of Feng Shui (pronounced 'fung shway') is 'Wind and Water'. These are the two elements that shape our very existence.

Originating in ancient China, Feng Shui is governed by principles based on 'ch'i', the fundamental energy force. As well as being present in the environment around us, ch'i also flows around the body through 'meridians'. The manipulation of these energy paths forms the basis of acupuncture, acupressure and shiatsu.

Our environment is constantly influenced by the invisible energy forces which affect our physical, emotional and spiritual health. Feng Shui enables us to balance and harness these energies to create a more favourable environment.

What energies are to be aligned?

There are three different sources of ch'i:

- Heaven's energy - or astrological energy - provides us with a source of guidance.

- Our own energy, stemming from the 'wind and water' (in the form of breath and blood) inside our body.

- The earth's energy, or the energy of our environment.

We can influence our own energy with a proper diet, discipline and meditation for our body, mind and spirit. The energy of our environment can be altered through Feng Shui tools such as colours, materials and shapes.

Yin and Yang

These are the two cosmic forces of energy which are opposite, yet complimentary. There is no balance in the universe without both of them. The forces of heaven are Yang and the forces of earth are Yin.

Yang is light, dry, loud, hard, full, hot, active, sun, fire, male, summer, day, and contracting, gathering, durable, horizontal, thicker and smaller.

Yin is dark, wet, quiet, soft, empty, cold, passive, moon, water, female, winter, night, expanding, dispersing, delicate, vertical, thinner and bigger.

For positive, auspicious Feng Shui there must be balance and harmony between Yin and Yang.

The Five Elements

Much of Feng Shui theory is based on understanding how these elements (earth, wood, fire, metal and water) interact in the physical environment, resulting in either harmony or imbalance.

In interior decor, the elements are represented by colours, shapes and materials. When an environment needs balancing, one way to solve the imbalance is to add or subtract the colour, shape or material that each element expresses

Element	Colour	Shapes	Material
Fire	Red	Pointed or triangular shapes, pyramids	Plastic, Diamonds
Earth	Yellow, Brown	Squares, flat shapes	Ceramics, Plaster, Clay, Bricks, China, Soft Stone
Metal	White, Gold, Silver	Spheres, circles, domes, arches, ovals, round shapes	Stainless Steel, Brass, Copper, Bronze, Iron, Silver, Gold, Marble
Water	Black, Blue	Wavy lines, irregular shapes	Glass
Wood	Green, Dark Green	Rectangular, tall, vertical shapes	Wood and Paper

Geopathic stress

Some negative earth energies can cause detrimental effects to the immune system and human psyche. 'Geopathic stress' can rise up through houses and cause occupants to lose physical strength, energy, emotional stability and happiness. It can also cause serious long-term illnesses.

Electromagnetic radiation from power transmission lines, radios, alarm clocks or bedside lights increases the effects of geopathic stress. Anything that disturbs the natural magnetic field of the earth (metal bed frames, beams, radiators, plumbing etc.) can cause sleep disturbance.

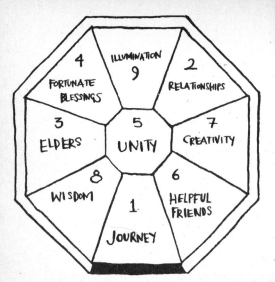

THE BAGUA GRID

How to use the Bagua Grid

Place the Bagua on top of the floor plan of your house in such a way that the front door of your house lines up with segments 8, 1 or 6 along the thick base line. You will then be able to identify the spaces in your home corresponding to all the areas of your life.

Remember that you can also place the Bagua over the plan of each room in the same way by lining up the door of each room with the thick line, to identify different areas of your life in each room.

AREA	NAME	RELATES TO YOUR
1	Journey	Career
2	Relationships	Love life/Marriage
3	Elders	Family/Ancestors/Past
4	Fortunate Blessings	Wealth/Prosperity
5	Unity	Health
6	Helpful Friends	Guidance/Mentors
7	Creativity	Children/New projects/Future
8	Wisdom	Knowledge
9	Illumination	Fame/Recognition

KEY TO THE BAGUA GRID

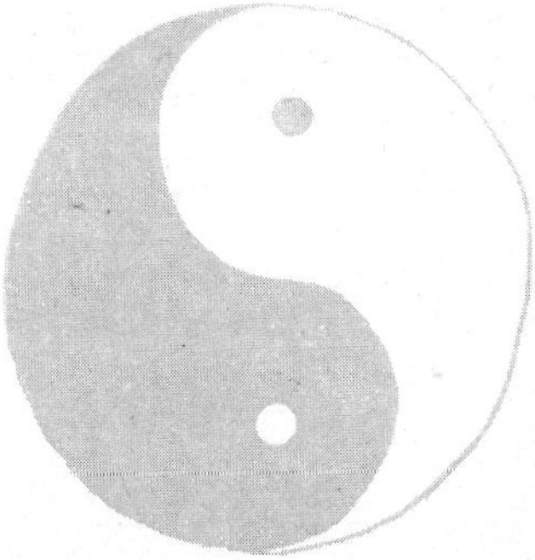

DUNWORRYIN

HOMEFRONT

BE PART OF NATURE

Greenery and wildlife in your neighbourhood are essential for your well-being and signify prosperity. Living in an area that is vibrant with birds, butterflies and foliage can be very beneficial. An alternative is to create a natural environment inside your home with large leafy plants, fresh flowers, nature landscapes and an indoor fountain.

KEEP AN OPEN PATH AHEAD

Ideally, front doors should not directly face large trees, tall buildings or telephone cable poles. They can attack your home with harmful negative energy, leading to stunted growth and poor health. To deflect this energy, hang a small Bagua-shaped mirror outside above your front door facing the object.

AVOID POISON ARROWS

Roads, rivers and bridges are conduits of energy. Negative energies from oncoming traffic or water pollution also act as 'poison arrows'. Shielding your front door with a fence, a hedge or a low wall will protect your home.

GET IT EVEN

The perfect shape for a home is a square or rectangle. Each corner or area of your house corresponds to a specific area of your life (e.g. relationships, career, health etc). If your house is uneven, problems can be caused in the aspect of your life corresponding to the area missing from the ideal square.

BRING IN SOME LIFE

One of the ways to rectify an uneven structure can be to hang a large mirror on the inside wall, facing inwards, behind the missing space. You can also square off the missing area by placement of potted plants, a bright light or a birdbath in the open space.

SECURE YOUR FORTRESS

Setting the boundaries for your home with a gate, a fence or a row of shrubs to mark out your territory increases your sense of security. Statues of animals such as lions on either side of the front gate offer protection, as does a bright light on your doorstep.

ALWAYS MOVE UP

For that 'uplifting' feeling, front doors should be approached either via an uphill slope or a few upward steps. Living in basements is inauspicious and should be avoided where possible.

UPLIFT YOUR FUTURE

Ensure that your house number is clearly marked so that visitors are not stressed when locating your home. Numbers should be placed climbing from left to right to keep your future optimistic.

THERE'S A LOT IN A NAME

Personalise your home with a meaningful name. Constantly look to improve its character with interesting objects in windows and flowering plants in your front path. The nicer the front of your home, the more you will benefit from the positive energies of those passing by.

PROJECT PLEASANT VIBRATIONS

Choose a pleasant sounding doorbell. Make sure it is always in working order. Your doorbell emits vibrations about you and should give a positive welcome to your guests.

ENTRANCE
HALL

FIRST IMPRESSIONS COUNT

The entrance hall is the transitional space from the outside world to your own and is a reflection of who you are. Have something inviting like an unusual water feature or a stunning work of art to focus the energy of your guests. This welcome will lift their ch'i and help them feel more relaxed.

WELCOME THE CH'I

Doors and windows control the movement of invisible ch'i. Ch'i entering the main door (the mouth of the house) gives you nourishment. Hence doors should always open 'into' the space. Windows (the eyes) should open 'out' like eyelids.

HARMONIZE THE ENTRANCE

Improve the quality of ch'i entering your home to enhance your well-being. Hanging a wind chime inside the doorway creates harmony by preventing negative ch'i and moderating the flow of positive ch'i.

CREATE AN INSTANT VISUAL IMPACT

Doors should open into the largest part of the room to create a feeling of space. Where this is not possible, place a large mirror close to the door, on the nearest wall to reflect the more spacious side of the room.

ENLARGE NARROW HALLS

Long and narrow entrance halls project a poor picture of your inner world. Feelings of limitation and rigidity, and even respiratory problems are common outcomes. Bright lighting, pale colours and a large mirror on the nearest wall create an impression of space.

EXPAND YOUR HORIZONS

An entrance door facing a blank wall can be oppressive and gives a sense of limited opportunities. Hanging a beautiful landscape with depth will give your soul a subliminal message of a pleasant journey ahead.

STOP LOSING THE CH'I

Your upper floor ch'i will escape if the staircase goes down to face the front door directly. Place a small mirror on the door facing the stairs to conserve the energy. Spiral stairs with open treads can also drain finances. Fill the treads and hang a wind chime in the middle of the stairway to slow the escape of ch'i.

CHOICE OF COLOUR

Colour makes a statement about you. It dominates your senses, interacts with your energies and alters perceptions. Use pale colours to instil a sense of calm and remember that white signifies purity and spaciousness.

LIVING ROOM

BRING NATURE INTO YOUR LIFE

Your living room is the space for relaxation, rest and socialising. Make it welcoming, comfortable and a visual feast for you and your visitors. Choose a spacious room with the best view outside to lift and replenish your ch'i.

DÉCOR TIPS

Choose the following for a supportive,
auspicious and balanced environment:

- Warm wall colour
- Matching furniture and curtain fabrics
- Soft, decorative floor rugs
- Exotic plants and fresh flowers
- Happy family photographs

GALLERY OUTLOOK

Living rooms mirror your personality, character and aspirations. Display your art collections, precious antiques and most loved objects against a natural background of plants and flowers. This will create a perfect balance of Yin and Yang and a harmonious environment.

FURNITURE DESIGN

Sharp edges or corners can be harmful because they create 'poison arrows' of negative energy. Rounded shapes and smooth edges stimulate a feeling of harmony and balance.

SETTING THE STAGE

Try to arrange the furniture in a way that minimises seats backing the doorway or windows. Keeping seats against solid walls gives everyone an increased sense of security and therefore puts them in a more relaxed mood.

ENTERTAIN IN STYLE

Ensure the seating arrangements for guests are cosy and close enough to stimulate conversation.

CREATE A COMFORT ZONE

While watching television, reading or listening to your favourite music, place your chair in the most convenient position in relation to the TV screen, the speakers or your garden. Keep tapes, CDs, books and your coffee table easily accessible.

IMPRESS YOUR GUESTS

Create a focal point with artistic objects (not your television!) Accentuate your fireplace with a painting or mirror above it. Even an exotic plant or a water feature in the wealth corner of the room will lift the ch'i instantly.

HANG SERENE IMAGES

Art is the medicine of the soul and raises your spirits. Select sculptures and images after carefully evaluating the types of messages they give. Serene landscapes with mountains, cascading water or a sunrise, for instance, give positive messages.

ENHANCE
STABILITY

Statues and sculptures add grace to any living room and provide stability. Place them in the spaces corresponding to the areas of your life needing greater support and security (see Bagua Grid). Place plants nearby for the contrast of Yin and Yang.

ENERGISE YOUR LOVE LIFE

A painting of lovers or an artistic or stone sculpture of a couple in the relationship area (see Bagua Grid) can impress your guests whilst also helping you find the right partner or even revive a flagging marriage. Pink peony flowers - a symbol of love - in a ceramic vase also activates romance.

ADD LIFE

Green plants represent growth. They help you stay healthy, clean the air, brighten dark corners and add life to any environment. Use large, leafy, upward-growing plants and not thorny cacti unless you want to be identified as a prickly person.

NEVER MIX BUSINESS WITH PLEASURE

Each space should be used for its intended activity. Living rooms are for resting. Working and leaving files or books there will prevent you from unwinding fully.

USE ADJUSTABLE LIGHTING

A dimmer switch is very useful for creating mood lighting for romance, serious reading or lively entertaining.

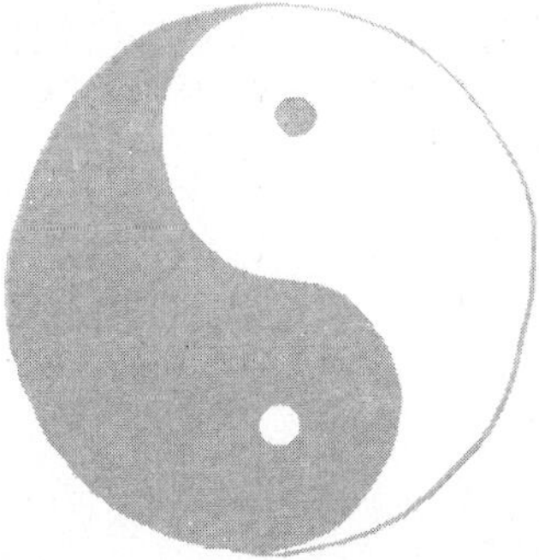

DINING ROOM

KEEP IT SIMPLE

Dining rooms have dual vibrations: the social energy of the living room and the nurturing energy of the kitchen. There is a fusion of intellect and nourishment. Avoid other distractions. Keep it clutter-free, supportive and simple.

GENTLE TOUCHES

For relaxed, informal gatherings, use the following:

- Lively and colourful mats, serviettes and flowers
- Comforting images
- Soft music
- Candles as a centrepiece

CONSERVE THE CH'I

A dining room can sometimes feel like a crossroads, often having doors from more than one room or being situated next to the kitchen or patio area. This may be disconcerting for diners, so do what you can to enclose the area to bring a sense of peace.

STABLE VIEWPOINT

Dining tables should be round, oval or octagonal with an even number of comfortable chairs. This makes the environment more harmonious and enhances the sense of fellowship. The host should always sit on a chair with a good view of the entrance to feel secure.

FUEL THE FIRE

A wooden dining table is preferable to a glass top or metal table. From an elemental perspective, a combination of wood and glass is positive, as glass represents water, which nourishes wood. Wood symbolises growth and fuels fire. Fire energy in Feng Shui refers to our destiny.

DOUBLE YOUR NOURISHMENT

Fresh flowers, fruit-filled bowls or colourful objects on the table add a new dimension to the décor. Hang a large mirror to reflect the dining table area. This signifies abundance of food.

KEEP YOUR LOVE ALIGHT

For a romantic dinner for two, use a pink tablecloth - the colour of love. A lit candle (symbolising passion) placed on a small mirror on the table will bring you closer.

GRACE

Take spiritual as well as physical nourishment from the occasion and the food by adding a sense of humility to meal times. Take a moment's silence before you eat. This will symbolise your gratitude to the divine power for what you are about to receive.

KITCHEN

ENERGY OF WEALTH

The kitchen contains the element of fire. The energy force here activates our wealth. It should be well designed, free of clutter and properly ventilated. Ideal locations are the fame or relationship areas of your home.

LIGHTING

Lighting should be a priority. People are healthier and more active when they work in well-lit areas. Dark corners are lifeless and consume twice as much of your energy. Adequate lighting will also enhance your culinary experience.

COLOURS DIGEST TOO

White is the best wall colour for a kitchen as it brings in more natural light and enhances purity and spaciousness. Yellow signifies earth energy that is nurturing, relaxing and warm. Red keeps you alert and should be avoided as it prevents good digestion.

KEEP IT NATURAL

Natural materials help you to relax quickly. Wood encourages a harmonious flow of energy. Baskets, cotton materials and plants will balance an environment full of shiny metallic objects and surfaces.

INAUSPICIOUS
LAYOUT

There should be a working triangle arrangement between the fridge, cooker and sink. Having the cooker (symbolic of the energy of fire) directly opposite the sink (the energy of water) can lead to arguments in the house.

AVOID SURPRISES

The cook should have a good view of the door. Where this is not possible, position a small mirror to be able to see if anyone is entering. This will prevent any subconscious insecurity whilst the meal is being prepared.

THE SINK

The sink should ideally be made of stainless steel, a symbol of prosperity and intuition. Locate it against a window overlooking a pleasant view. Keep it clean and unblocked as the plumbing relates to your intestines.

ONE WAY TRAFFIC

The fridge should be white, or concealed in a wooden unit. Disguise it to help you diet or stick a symbol of a 'no entry' road sign to the fridge door. Food magnets may increase the tendency to think about eating too much of the time.

PEACE AND QUIET

Extractor fans are undesirable. Open the window instead to let the fresh ch'i come in. Peaceful, nourishing and sacred space should ideally not have noise pollution from any equipment.

ENSURE EVERYTHING WORKS

Broken gadgets around you weaken your energy levels. Be it a light bulb, a radio, an electric mixer or your dishwasher, fix it or throw it out.

BITS AND BOBS

- Use lino, wood, or cleaner-friendly floor tiles.
- Never use bins without lids.
- Keep knives out of sight to avoid cutting ch'i.
- Have rounded corners on all units and worktops for good health.

PRESERVE
NUTRITIONAL VALUES...

A microwave is a non-starter. Research shows that food cooked in this way does not help in a speedy recovery from ill health. Use it if you must, with plants nearby to absorb its electromagnetic radiation.

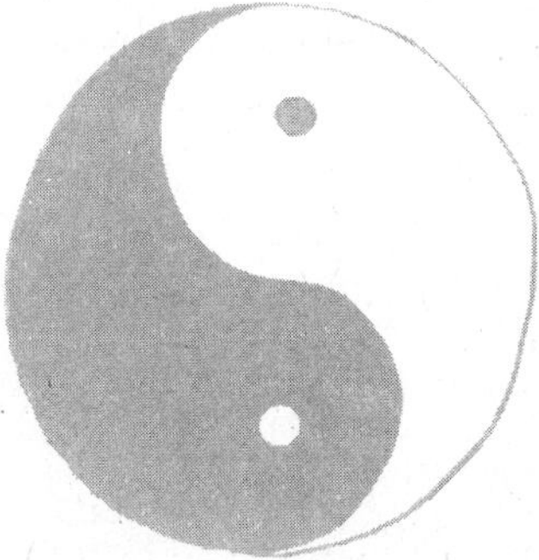

STUDY

KNOWING YOURSELF

Your study represents the space containing the energy of knowledge, influencing your wisdom. It enriches the relationship with 'yourself'. Keep it clutter-free, organised and vibrant. Your study should ideally be in the wisdom area of your home.

SAFE ARRANGEMENT

Position your desk against a solid wall with a diagonal view of the door and window. Avoid walkway spaces or shelving behind you. Such auspicious arrangement stimulates focused thinking and provides a safe, supportive environment.

CREATE A PARADISE

Changing the outer landscape transforms your inner landscape. Surround yourself with inspiring pieces that remind you of your goals.

SIT LIKE A KING

Your chair governs your alignment between heaven and earth's energy forces. It should have a high back, curved lower back, seat tilt, and be height adjustable and have armrests, all of which keep you at an optimum balance.

AVOID SLIPPERY EGDES

When the element wood is used in a desk it signifies authority and growth. Non-reflective surfaces in natural, light wood or muted colours are ideal for optimum focus.

- Rounded, oval or arc horseshoe shapes stimulate creativity.
- Square shapes with rounded corners are auspicious for work with figures.
- Rectangle shapes let your money slip away.

PLANT PROTECTION

Computers, stereo systems, digital clocks and mobile telephones emit electromagnetic pollution harmful to our well-being. Plants absorb and counteract this energy. Palms, peace lilies and spider plants are ideal.

CRYSTAL CLEAR REMEDY

Sit at least three feet away from the back of your computer. The electromagnetic rays can penetrate the meridians through exposed skin and deteriorate the quality of your blood. Placing a raw crystal on the terminal would neutralise the negative energy field and strengthen your intuition.

WINDOW DRESSINGS

For an aesthetically uplifting ambience
and to foster clear thinking, always use:

- Pale colours for walls (green or blue)
- A bright up-lighter plus a desk lamp
  if required
- Low level shelving for books

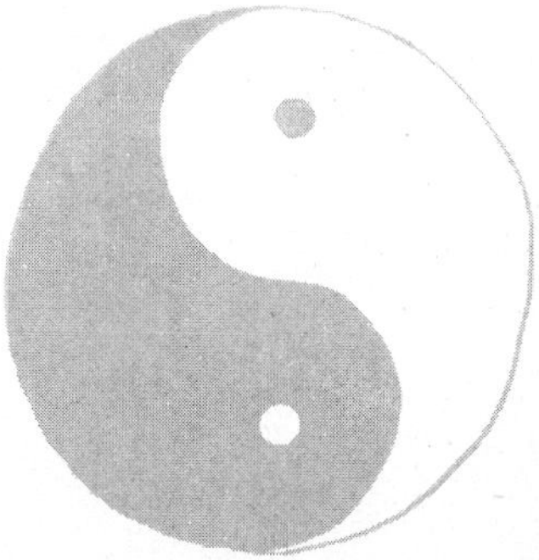

BATHROOM

WATER IS WEALTH

The bathroom is governed by the element of water, closely related to money and emotions. Any leak or drip in the sink, tub, shower or toilet will imply loss of 'money energy' and 'emotional strength' and should be fixed immediately.

LOCATION MATTERS

The most suitable location for your bathroom is the area of elders. A bathroom facing the front door drains you by giving your brain a false signal, making you use it more frequently than necessary. Placing a mirror on the outside of the bathroom door will help. Keep the bathroom door shut at all times.

AVOID MORNING TRAFFIC JAMS

Ideally, separate bathrooms and toilets for better hygiene and for eliminating queues!

AVOID CONFRONTATION

A bathroom facing the kitchen can create more arguments with the combative positions of water energy with fire energy. Hang a crystal in the middle of the kitchen to adjust this imbalance.

WORST SCENARIO

Bathrooms in the wealth area will impact on your ability to generate and hold on to your money. 'Wealth ch'i' will be flushed away. Keep the lavatory lid shut. Place a small hardy plant in the windowsill to retain the water energy.

LESS IS MORE

Shelves, windowsills, the floor even the bathtub rim should be c free. This facilitates cleaning makes the room calm and pea Keep a small plant like a fern to s the environment.

POLICY MATTER

The holes in the sink and the bathtub are the escape routes of ch'i. Form a habit of plugging them, when not in use. This will prevent energy in the bathroom from draining away.

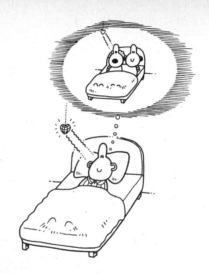

BEDROOM

BEST LOCATION

The main bedroom should ideally be at the back of the home, to the far right of the main door, overlooking a pleasant view. This area represents your relationship corner.

DÉCOR TIPS

- Soft materials and furnishings are very relaxing.
- Pale blue walls are calming. Add touches of red for love.
- A large plant freshens the room.
- Candles represent passion.
- Rounded furniture stimulates romance.

IDEAL BED LOCATION

While sleeping, always have a view of the doorway. However, never sleep directly facing one. The powerful energy force entering the door can cause health problems by weakening your own ch'i. Sleep with a solid wall behind you for an increased sense of security.

ARE YOU SLEEPING IN A SAFE PLACE?

If you frequently feel uneasy or tired and suffer from health problems or insomnia, then your bedroom may be suffering from geopathic stress. Check this out in your bedroom by calling an expert to analyse and rectify the situation.

TOGETHERNESS

Couples should sleep on a double bed. Sleeping in two separate beds or one bed with two single mattresses suggests an unstable relationship and can lead to separation.

STRENGTHEN YOUR SUPPORT

A solid headboard is a must. This gives an increased sense of support and nourishment to your head. A round one is preferable to a square one. Wooden or padded ones can create a more romantic mood.

A WORD OF CAUTION

Avoid positioning your bed under a beam or a sloping ceiling. Beams can cause rifts in relationships and lead to poor health, whereas slopes push energy down on top of you making you feel oppressed. If relocation of your bed is impossible, disguise the beam by painting it the same colour as the ceiling to render it less harmful.

UP...UP... AND AWAY...

Good lighting, melodious sounds and pleasant images create positive vibrations. The energy of the room may be lifted with the use of up-lighters, soft music, and beautiful landscapes.

OVERHANGING FEAR

Hanging pictures on the wall above your headboard creates vibrations of fear and anxiety and can affect the quality of your sleep.

CLEAR THE CLUTTER

Clutter in your room is the biggest enemy of Feng Shui and emits chaotic vibrations that result in unclear thinking. Are you aware that you spend a third of your life in this room? Keep it neat and tidy at all times.

DON'T HANG ON TO THINGS

Piles of old magazines and unwanted books create stagnant energy. Only keep items of value. Let go of the past to make room for the future. Revitalise your energy.

CLEAR YOUR WARDROBE

Most of the time, we tend to wear the same 20% of our clothes. Keep only the items which you use and love - give the rest away

DRESSING TABLE RULES

Do not display your entire collection of toiletries on your dressing table. Keep only the items you frequently use. This will prevent the formation of stagnant ch'i in your most sacred sanctuary - your bedroom.

BEDROOM MIRRORS

Mirrors are an integral part of any bedroom and sometimes they are placed alongside or over the bed to spice up your sex life. Mirrors reflecting your bed will drain your energy even during your sleep. They tend to act as a stimulant, making it difficult for you to rest and relax. To wake up feeling fresh and lively, place mirrors inside wardrobes or cover them with thin curtains while you sleep.

BEDSIDE TABLE MANNERS

Keep bedside tables clutter free: you can only read one book at a time. Switch off the bedside lamps from the wall sockets every night. Electromagnetic vibrations entering your body's aura are harmful and they linger if the wall socket switch is left on.

DO NOT MIX ENERGIES

Desks, computers or bookshelves belong in a study. Televisions, clock radios and answering machines lower the quality of your sleep with their electromagnetic pollution. Avoid them or keep them at least eight feet away from your head.

ALWAYS HAVE A PAIR

Your pictures and sculptures are all symbolic. Solitary sculptures and images give messages of solitude as a way of life to your subconscious mind. Happy relationships can be enhanced by pictures of pairs (e.g. couples in paintings, sculptures or photographs).

ADD A SPARKLE

Check the relationship corner of the room on the far right from the door. Keep it tidy. Hang a sparkling heart shaped crystal to keep it energized and romantic.

CHERISH YOUR UNION

To enrich your emotional and physical union, place photographs of the two of you together and a pair of ceramic doves, dolphins or mandarin ducks in the relationship corner of your room. Ducks in general are known to enjoy monogamous relationships in their lives. This can cultivate your desires to give you a healthy sex life.

KID'S
BEDROOM

INSTIL THE PRINCIPLE OF GENEROSITY

Clutter can block your children's ability to think clearly. They can become confused and distracted. Unnecessary or unwanted toys, books and clothes should be donated to charity.

DÉCOR TIPS

Bedrooms shape children's dreams and destinies by stimulating and nurturing their ch'i. Locate their rooms in the creativity area of your home. Ensure that the room has:

- Soft wall colours
- Bright lights and a nice window
- Uplifting colours in posters and paintings
- At least one plant with rounded leaves
- No dried flowers
- Some personal identity on the door

BED PLACEMENT

Ensure that your child sleeps:

- In a corner, to get maximum support from the walls
- Without any overhanging furniture for good health
- In full view of, but not directly facing the door, for enhanced security

NEVER CONSTRAIN
THE SPACE

Bunk beds are undesirable. The overhang of the upper bed can limit the growth potential of the child in the lower bunk. The upper bed, being in close proximity to the ceiling is also oppressive and cuts down the energy flow around the body.

ADD GENTLENESS

Curtains or roller blinds are preferable to the traditional horizontal or vertical blinds which create harmful cutting ch'i when open. A soft, spacious and fresh environment stimulates creativity. Use pillows and cuddly toys where appropriate.

THEY DON'T HAVE
GIRAFFE NECKS

Artwork should hang at eye level. Children should not strain themselves to appreciate it. Their comfort should be our priority. After all, this room is their personal space.

CENSOR THE IMAGES

Each poster or painting carries a
vibration with a subliminal message
which moulds a child's character.
Eliminate any images giving
undesirable vibrations.

FEEL SAFE

Desks should be placed diagonally facing the door and not block the flow of energy entering the room. With the doorway in full view, children feel safer and more secure.

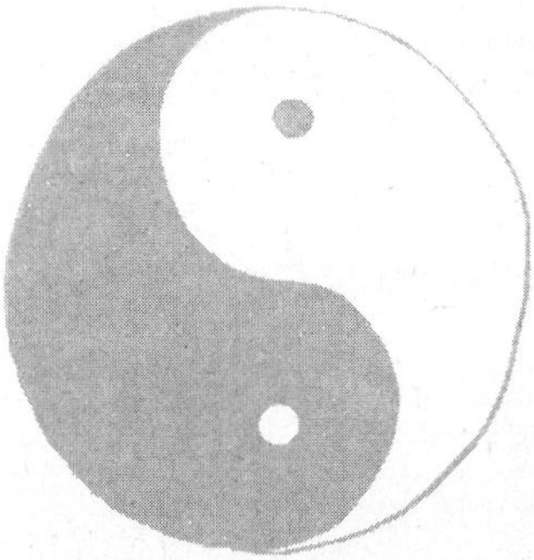

GARDEN

A SACRED PLACE

A garden is an outdoor sacred room that speaks to your soul. A view of nature provides fresh inner peace and inspiration and can calm your stressful emotions.

MEANDERING LIKE A
LAZY RIVER

Lush vegetation, elevated hillocks, curving paths with boulders on either side and carefully placed rockeries will attract butterflies, bees and birds and also prevent the energies relating to health and finance from slipping away.

STRIKE A BALANCE

Lift your ch'i and nourish your physical, emotional and spiritual levels with a combination of sunlight and shade. Place your garden chairs under the shade of a parasol or vine-covered trellis.

NURTURE YOUR LOVE LIFE

Place an arbour in the relationship corner of your garden. Keep a sculpture of a couple nearby and grow fragrant flowers around it to lift your romantic energy and strengthen your partnership.

FOUNTAIN OF HEALTH
AND WEALTH

The sight and sound of flowing water is therapeutic for your health. A flowing stream, water fountain or rocky waterfall in the wealth corner of the garden revitalizes the area and enhances prosperity. A fishpond or a birdbath is auspicious too.

FOLIAGE, WALLS
AND FENCES

- Foliage planted near brick walls and fences creates a balance between yin and yang and adds harmony to the landscape.
- Avoid pointed fences to eliminate harmful cutting ch'i.

HEALING MYSTICISM

- Create an ambience of healing, contemplation and meditation by planting aromatic shrubs, herbs and vegetables.
- Meandering pathways with colourful flowers add a sense of mysticism.

GLOSSARY

Aura - Energy field outside all living bodies.

Bagua - Octagonal grid used to locate the various sectors of your life in your home.

Ch'i - Cosmic energy force which exists in the environment, underground and within us.

Clutter - Things which you possess but neither use nor love.

Cutting Ch'i - (Also known as poison arrow) Inauspicious energy line emanating from a sharp, pointed object or structure.

Feng Shui - 'Wind and water'. It is the art of balancing the environment and living in harmony.

Five elements - Water, wood, fire, soil and metal.

Geopathic stress - The effect of negative earth energies detrimental to your well-being.

Harmony - Bliss.

Poison Arrow - See Cutting Ch'i.

Relationship corner - Far right area of your home from the front door corresponding to your love life or marriage.

Wealth corner - Far left area of your home from the front door corresponding to prosperity.

Yin and Yang - Two opposite and complementary types of cosmic energy forces. Yin is dark, passive and receptive energy. Yang is light, positive and creative energy.